On-the-Go FASHIONS™
for 18-inch Dolls
JENNY KING

Contents

Runway Fashion Vest

SKILL LEVEL

INTERMEDIATE

FINISHED MEASUREMENT
10½ inches in diameter

MATERIALS

- Plymouth Encore Tweed medium (worsted) weight acrylic/wool/rayon yarn (3½ oz/200 yds/100g per ball):
  1 ball #T461 grape jam
- Size H/8/5mm crochet hook or size needed to obtain gauge
- Tapestry needle
- Stitch marker

GAUGE
8 sts = 2 inches; 6 rows = 2 inches

PATTERN NOTES
Join with slip stitch as indicated unless otherwise stated.

Chain-3 at beginning of round counts as first double crochet unless otherwise stated.

Chain-2 at beginning of round counts as first half double crochet unless otherwise stated.

VEST
Row 1: Ch 18, sc in 2nd ch from hook, sc in each rem ch across, turn. *(17 sc)*

Rows 2–13: Ch 1, working in **front lps** *(see Stitch Guide)*, sc in each st across, turn.

ARMHOLE SHAPING
Rnd 13: Now working in rnds, ch 4 *(armhole made)*, sc in first ch on opposite side of foundation ch, sc in each rem ch across, ch 4 *(armhole made)*, sc in each st across row 13, **join** *(see Pattern Notes)* in first ch of beg ch-4, turn. *(42 sts)*

Rnd 14: **Ch 3** *(see Pattern Notes)*, dc in same st, dc in each of next 6 sts, [2 dc in next st, dc in each of next 6 sts] 5 times, join in 3rd ch of beg ch-3. *(48 sts)*

Continued on page 20

Paris Bound

SKILL LEVEL

INTERMEDIATE

FINISHED MEASUREMENTS

Dress: 10 inches long

Beret: 4¾ inches in diameter

Bag: 4½ inches tall, without fringe or strap

MATERIALS
- Plymouth Gina medium (worsted) weight wool yarn (1¾ oz/109 yds/ 50g per ball):
  3 balls #0006 green/gray/purple variegated
- Sizes 7/4.5mm and J/10/6mm crochet hooks or size needed to obtain gauge
- Tapestry needle
- Stitch marker

GAUGE

Size J hook: 14 sc = 4 inches; 16 rows = 4 inches

PATTERN NOTES

Dress and Bag are worked in continuous rounds; do not turn or join unless otherwise stated.

Beret is worked in joined rounds; do not turn unless otherwise stated. Ribbing is worked in continuous rounds; do not turn or join unless otherwise stated.

Mark first stitch of round.

Weave in ends as work progresses.

Join with slip stitch as indicated unless otherwise stated.

Chain-3 at beginning of round counts as first double crochet unless otherwise stated.

DRESS

Rnd 1: With size J hook, ch 36, **join** (*see Pattern Notes*) in first ch to form ring, ch 1, sc in each ch around. (*36 sc*)

Rnds 2–12: Sc in each sc around.

ARMHOLE SHAPING
Rnd 13: Sc in next 12 sts, ch 8 *(armhole made)*, sk next 6 sts, sc in next 12 sts, ch 8 *(armhole made)*, sk next 6 sts.

Rnd 14: [Sc in next 12 sts, 8 sc in next ch-8 sp] twice.

Rnds 15–40: Sc in each st around. At end of last rnd, fasten off.

BERET
Rnd 1: With size 7 hook, ch 5, **join** *(see pattern Notes)* in first ch to form ring, **ch 3** *(see Pattern Notes)*, 11 dc in ring, join in 3rd ch of beg ch-3. *(12 dc)*

Rnd 2: Ch 3, dc in first st, 2 dc in each rem st around, join in 3rd ch of beg ch-3. *(24 dc)*

Rnd 3: Ch 3, dc in first st, dc in next st, [2 dc in next st, dc in the next st] 11 times, join in 3rd ch of beg ch-3. *(36 dc)*

Rnd 4: Ch 3, dc in first st, dc in each of next 2 sts, [2 dc in next st, dc in each of next 2 sts] 11 times, join in 3rd ch of beg ch-3. *(48 dc)*

Rnd 5: Ch 3, dc in each st around, join in 3rd ch of beg ch-3.

Rnd 6: Ch 3, dc in next st, **dc dec** *(see Stitch Guide)* in next 2 sts, [dc in each of next 2 sts, dc dec in next 2 sts] 11 times, join in 3rd ch of beg ch-3. *(36 sts)*

RIBBING
Rnds 7–11: Working in **back lps** *(see Stitch Guide)*, sc in each st around.

Fasten off.

BAG
Rnd 1: With size 7 hook, ch 5, **join** *(see Pattern Notes)* in first ch to form ring, 10 sc in ring. *(10 sc)*

Rnd 2: 2 sc in each st around. *(20 sc)*

Rnd 3: Sc in each st around.

Rnd 4: 2 sc in first st, sc in next st, [2 sc in next st, sc in next st] 9 times. *(30 sc)*

Rnds 5–15: [Rep rnd 3] 11 times.

Rnd 16: Sc in each of next 3 sts, **sc dec** *(see Stitch Guide)* in next 2 sts, [sc next 3 sts, sc dec in next 2 sts] 5 times. *(24 sts)*

Rnds 17 & 18: Working in **back lps** *(see Stitch Guide)*, sc in each st around.

STRAP
Row 1: Now working in rows, ch 3, dc in last st of rnd 18, [ch 3, dc in last dc] 11 times, sk next 12 sts of rnd 18, join in next st. Fasten off.

FRINGE
Cut 8 strands of yarn, each 6 inches long. Fold strands in half. Insert hook from 1 side of rnd 1, through bag, to the other side of rnd 1. Draw fold through bag, insert ends of strands through folded end and pull loose ends to tighten fringe. ■

Today's Cowgirl

SKILL LEVEL

INTERMEDIATE

FINISHED MEASUREMENTS

Cardigan: 7½ inches long

Top: 5¼ inches long

Skirt: 5¼ inches long

Bag: 2¼ inches x 3¾ inches, without strap

MATERIALS

- Omega Mimosa fine (sport) weight cotton/rayon yarn (3½ oz/240 yds/ 100g per skein): **2 FINE**
    1 skein #83 lime
- Omega Trigo light (light worsted) weight cotton yarn (3½ oz/295 yds/ 100g per ball): **3 LIGHT**
    1 ball each #283 olive, #291 ash and #224 taupe
- Sizes E/4/3.5mm and G/6/4mm crochet hooks or size needed to obtain gauge
- Tapestry needle
- Stitch markers: 4
- ¾-inch buttons: 3

GAUGE

With size G hook and 1 strand lime and olive held tog: 16 dc = 4 inches; 7 rows = 4 inches

PATTERN NOTES

Cardigan is worked in turned rows from top down with raglan shaping to armhole, then in joined rounds.

Place marker in each chain-5 loop as stated in row 1 of Cardigan. Move marker up as work progresses.

Join with slip stitch as indicated unless otherwise stated.

Top is worked in turned rows with 1 strand of each yarn held together. Front is worked from waist to shoulder then Back is worked on either side of Front.

Chain-3 at beginning of row counts as first double crochet unless otherwise stated.

Chain-2 at beginning of row counts as first single crochet and chain-1 unless otherwise stated.

Chain-4 at beginning of round counts as first double crochet and chain-1 unless otherwise stated.

Bag is worked in turned rows and folded in half; sides are then crocheted together.

Weave in ends as work progresses.

SPECIAL STITCHES
Shell: (Sc, ch 3, 3 dc) as indicated in instructions.

Cluster (cl): Holding back last lp of each st on hook, 5 tr in indicated st or sp, yo, draw through all 6 lps on hook.

CARDIGAN
Row 1: With size G hook and lime, ch 38, sc in 2nd ch from hook, ch 5, sc in next ch, **place marker** *(see Pattern Notes)* in previous ch-5 lp, [ch 5, sk next 3 chs, sc in next ch] twice, ch 5, sc in next ch, place marker in previous ch-5 lp, [ch 5, sk next 3 chs, sc in next ch] 4 times, ch 5, sc in next ch, place marker in previous ch-5 lp, [ch 5, sk next 3 chs, sc in next ch] twice, ch 3, dc in last ch, place marker in previous ch-3 lp, turn. *(12 sc, 1 dc, 8 ch-5 lps, 4 marked lps)*

Row 2: Ch 5, sc in first marked lp, [ch 5, sc in next ch-5 lp] twice, ch 5, (sc, ch 5, sc) in next marked lp, [ch 5, sc in next ch-5 lp] 4 times, ch 5, (sc, ch 5, sc) in next marked lp, [ch 5, sc in next ch-5 lp] twice, ch 5, (sc, ch 3, dc) in last marked lp, turn. *(14 sc, 1 dc, 11 ch-5 lps, 4 marked lps)*

Row 3: Ch 5, sc in first marked lp, [ch 5, sc in next ch-5 lp] 3 times, ch 5, (sc, ch 5, sc) in next marked ch-5 lp, [ch 5, sc in next ch-5 lp] 5 times, ch 5, (sc, ch 5, sc) in next marked ch-5 lp, [ch 5, sc in next ch-5 lp] 3 times, ch 5, (sc, ch 3, dc) in last marked lp, turn. *(17 sc, 1 dc, 14 ch-5 lps, 4 marked lps)*

Row 4: Ch 5, sc in first marked lp, [ch 5, sc in next ch-5 lp] 4 times, ch 5, (sc, ch 5, sc) in next marked ch-5 lp, [ch 5, sc in next ch-5 lp] 6 times, ch 5, (sc, ch 5, sc) in next marked ch-5 lp, [ch 5, sc in next ch-5 lp] 4 times, ch 5, (sc, ch 3, dc) in last marked ch-5 lp, turn. *(20 sc, 1 dc, 16 ch-5 lps, 4 marked lps)*

ARMHOLE SHAPING
Row 5: Ch 1, sc in first marked lp, sk next 5 ch-5 lps, sc in next marked lp *(armhole made)*, [ch 5, sc in next ch-5 lp] 7 times, ch 5, sc in next marked lp, sk next 5 ch-5 lps, sc in last marked lp *(armhole made)*, turn. *(11 sc, 8 ch-5 lps)*

Note: *Following rnds are worked in continuous rnds. Do not join unless specified; mark beg of rnds.*

Rnd 6: Now working in rnds, [ch 5, sc in next ch-5 lp] 23 times evenly sp around entire piece, ch 2, dc in first ch. *(24 ch-5 lps)*

Rnds 7–11: [Ch 5, sc in next ch-5 lp] 23 times, ch 2, dc in last dc.

Rnd 12: Ch 5, (sc, ch 5, sc) in next ch-5 lp, [ch 5, sc in next ch-5 lp, ch 5, (sc, ch 5, sc) in next ch-5 lp] 10 times, ch 5, sc in next ch-5 lp, ch 5, (sc, ch 5, sc) in next ch-5 lp, ch 2, dc in last dc. *(36 ch-5 lps)*

Rnd 13: [Ch 5, sc in next ch-5 lp] 35 times, ch 2, dc in last dc.

Rnd 14: Ch 1, sc in first ch-5 lp, [5 dc in next ch-5 lp, sc in next ch-5 lp] 17 times, 5 dc in last ch-2 lp, **join** *(see Pattern Notes)* in first sc. Fasten off.

SLEEVES
Rnd 1: Join lime with sc in any ch-5 lp of underarm, [ch 5, sc in next ch-5 lp] 4 times, ch 2, dc in first sc. *(5 lps)*

Rnds 2–6: [Ch 5, sc in next ch-5 lp] 4 times, ch 2, dc in next dc.

Rnd 7: [Ch 5, (sc, ch 5, sc) in next ch-5 lp] 5 times, join in first ch. *(10 ch-5 lps)*

Rnd 8: Ch 1, 5 sc in each ch-5 lp around, join in first sc. Fasten off. *(50 sts)*

Rep for 2nd Sleeve.

TOP
FRONT
Row 1: With size G hook and with 1 strand olive and 1 strand lime held tog, ch 22, dc in 4th ch from hook *(sk 3 chs count as first dc)*, dc in each rem ch across, turn. *(20 dc)*

Rows 2–8: Ch 3 *(see Pattern Notes)*, working in **front lps** *(see Stitch Guide)*, dc in each st across, turn.

Row 9: Ch 3, dc in each of next 3 dc, sl st in each of next 12 sts, dc in each of last 4 sts. Fasten off lime only.

BACK
FIRST SIDE
Note: *Turn the work clockwise 90 degrees and work down the side of the front.*

Row 1: With size E hook and 1 strand olive, sc in top of the last st worked in row 9, ch 10 *(armhole made)*, sk next 4 rows, [sc, ch 1] 6 times evenly sp across next 5 rows, sc in last row, turn. *(8 sc, 1 ch-10 sp, 6 ch-1 sps)*

Row 2: Ch 2 *(see Pattern Notes)*, *sk next sc, sc in next ch-1 sp, ch 1, rep from * across to ch-10 sp, [sc, ch 1] 5 times in ch-10 sp, sc in last sc, turn.

Rows 3–15: Ch 2, *sk next sc, sc in next ch-1 sp, ch 1, rep from * across to beg ch-2 sp, sc in beg ch-2 sp. Fasten off.

2ND SIDE
Rows 1–12: With size E hook, join olive in first st of row 9, rep rows 1–12 of First Side.

Row 13: Ch 2, sk next sc, *sc in next ch-1 sp, ch 3, sk next 3 sts *(buttonhole made)*, [sc in next ch-1 sp, ch 1, sk next sc] twice, rep from * twice,

[sc in next ch-1 sp, ch 1, sk next sc] twice, sc in beg ch-2 sp, turn.

Row 14: Ch 2, sk next sc, *(sc, ch 1, sc) in next ch-3 sp, [ch 1, sk next sc, sc in next ch-1 sp] twice, ch 1, rep from * once, (sc, ch 1, sc) in next ch-3 sp, ch 1, sk next sc, sc in next sc, ch 1, sc in beg ch-2 sp. Fasten off.

FINISHING
Sew shoulder seams. Sew buttons opposite buttonholes.

SKIRT
Rnd 1: With size E hook and 1 strand lime, ch 44, **join** *(see Pattern Notes)* in first ch to form ring, **ch 4** *(see Pattern Notes)*, sk next ch, [dc in next ch, ch 1, sk next ch] 21 times, join in 3rd ch of beg ch-4. Fasten off.

Rnd 2: Join olive in first ch-1 sp, ch 1, **shell** *(see Special Stitches)* in same sp, [sk next 3 sts, shell in next st, sk next 3 sts, shell in next ch-1 sp] 14 times, join in first sc, turn. Fasten off.

Rnd 3: Join taupe in first ch-3 sp, shell in same sp, shell in each rem ch-3 sp around, join in first sc, turn. Fasten off.

Rnd 4: With ash, rep rnd 3.

Rnd 5: With olive, rep rnd 3.

Rnd 6: With taupe, rep rnd 3.

Rnd 7: With ash, rep rnd 3.

Rnd 8: With olive, rep rnd 3.

Rnd 9: With taupe, rep rnd 3.

Rnd 10: With ash, rep rnd 3.

TIE
With lime, ch 70. Fasten off.

FINISHING
Thread Tie through ch-1 sps on rnd 1 of Skirt. Knot each end of Tie.

Continued on page 21

Snuggly Bear Romper & Hood

FINISHED MEASUREMENTS
Romper: 16 inches long

Hood: 6 inches tall

MATERIALS
- Plymouth Encore Tweed medium (worsted) weight acrylic/wool/rayon yarn (3½ oz/200 yds/100g per ball): 2 balls #1237 granola
- Sizes F/5/3.75mm, G/6/4mm and J/10/6mm crochet hooks or size needed to obtain gauge
- Tapestry needle
- 1½-inch button

GAUGE
Size J hook: 14 sc = 4 inches; 15 rows = 4 inches

PATTERN NOTES
Romper is worked in continuous rounds; do not turn or join unless otherwise stated.

Mark first stitch of round.

Join with slip stitch as indicated unless otherwise stated.

Weave in ends as work progresses.

Chain-4 at beginning of round counts as first treble crochet unless otherwise stated.

Chain-2 at beginning of row counts as first single crochet and chain-1 unless otherwise stated.

ROMPER
NECK
Rnd 1: With size J hook, ch 36, **join** (*see Pattern Notes*) in first ch to form ring, ch 1, sc in each ch around. (*36 sc*)

Rnd 2: Sc in each sc around.

ARMHOLE SHAPING
Rnd 3: Sc in each of next 12 sc, ch 10 (*armhole made*), sk next 6 sc, sc in each of next 12 sc, ch 10 (*armhole made*), sk next 6 sc.

BODY
Rnd 4: Sc in each of next 12 sc, sc in each of next 10 chs, sc in each of next 12 sc, sc in each of next 10 chs. (*44 sc*)

Rnds 5–25: Rep rnd 2.

FIRST LEG
Rnd 26: Sc in each of next 22 sts, leaving rem sts unworked. (*22 sts*)

Rnds 27–46: Working on 22 sts of rnd 26, sc in each st around.

FOOT
Row 47: Now working in rows with size G hook, sc in each of next 8 sts, leaving rem sts unworked, turn. (*8 sts*)

Rows 48–51: Ch 1, sc in each st across, turn.

Row 52: Ch 1, sk first st, sc in each of next 5 sts, **sc dec** (*see Stitch Guide*) in next 2 sts. (*6 sts*)

Rnd 53: Now working in rnds, sc evenly sp along side of row 52 of Foot, [sc dec in next 2 sts] 7 times around unworked sts of rnd 46 of Leg, sc evenly sp along opposite side of row 52, sc in each st of row 52. (*20 sc*)

Rnds 54–58: Sc in each st around. Leaving an 8-inch tail for sewing, fasten off.

2ND LEG
Join yarn in first unworked st on rnd 25 of Body, rep as for First Leg and Foot.

SLEEVES

Rnd 1: With size J hook, join yarn in first st of armhole, work 18 sc evenly sp around armhole. *(18 sts)*

Rnds 2–17: Sc in each st around.

Rnds 18–20: With size F hook, sc in each st around. Fasten off.

Rep for 2nd Sleeve.

CORD

With size F hook, ch 80. Fasten off.

HOOD

Row 1: With size J hook, ch 12, sc in 2nd ch from hook, sc in each ch across to last ch, 3 sc in last ch, working across opposite side of foundation ch, sc in each ch across, turn. *(23 sc)*

Row 2: Ch 1, sc in each of first 11 sts, 3 sc in next st, sc in each rem st across, turn. *(25 sc)*

Row 3: Ch 1, sc in each of first 12 sts, 3 sc in next st, sc in each rem st across, turn. *(27 sc)*

Rows 4–21: Ch 1, sc in each st across, turn.

Rows 22 & 23: Ch 11, sc in 2nd ch from hook, sc in each rem ch and st across, turn. *(37 sc, 47 sc)*

Row 24: Ch 1, sc in each of first 2 sts, ch 2, sk next 2 sts *(buttonhole made)*, sc in each rem st across, turn.

Row 25: Ch 1, sc in each st across to ch-2 sp, 2 sc in ch-2 sp, sc in each of last 2 sts, turn.

Fasten off.

EARS
Make 2.

Rnd 1: Ch 5, sl st in first ch to form ring, **ch 4** *(see Pattern Notes)*, 7 tr in ring. *(8 tr)*

Leaving 6-inch tail for sewing, fasten off.

Continued on page 21

Très Chic Ensemble

SKILL LEVEL

■■■▭
INTERMEDIATE

FINISHED MEASUREMENTS

Coat: 11 inches long

Leggings: 4¾ inches tall

Hat: 4½ inches in diameter

MATERIALS

- Plymouth Encore Tweed medium (worsted) weight acrylic/wool/rayon yarn (3½ oz/200 yds/100g per ball): 2 balls #5539 pink
- Sizes 7/4.5mm and J/10/6mm crochet hooks or size needed to obtain gauge
- Tapestry needle
- Stitch marker
- 1-inch buttons: 3

GAUGE

Size J hook: 17 sts = 4 inches; 17 rows = 4 inches

PATTERN NOTES

Jacket is worked in 2 pieces, each from center back to front.

Sleeves are worked in turned rounds after back, collar and shoulders are seamed.

Weave in ends as work progresses.

Chain-2 at beginning of row or round counts as first single crochet and chain-1 unless otherwise stated.

Join with slip stitch as indicated unless otherwise stated.

COAT
FIRST SIDE
Row 1: With size J hook, ch 40, sc in 4th ch from hook, ch 1, *sk next ch, sc in next ch, ch 1, rep from * across to last ch, sc in last ch, turn. *(19 sc)*

Row 2: Ch 2 *(see Pattern Notes)*, *sk next sc, sc in next ch-1 sp, ch 1, rep from * across to sp formed by beg 3 sk chs, sc in sp, turn.

Rows 3–13: Ch 2, *sk next sc, sc in next ch-1 sp, ch 1, rep from * across to beg ch-2 sp, sc in beg ch-2 sp, turn.

Row 14: Ch 2, [sk next sc, sc in next ch-1 sp, ch 1] 13 times, sk next st, sc in next st, leaving rem sts unworked, turn.

ARMHOLE SHAPING
Row 15: Ch 14 *(armhole made)*, sc in 4th ch from hook, ch 1, [sk next ch, sc in next ch, ch 1] 5 times, *sk next sc, sc in next ch-1 sp, ch 1, rep from * across to beg ch-2 sp, sc in beg ch-2 sp, turn.

Row 16: Ch 2, *sk next sc, sc in next ch-1 sp, ch 1, rep from * across to sp formed by beg 3 sk chs, sc in sp, turn.

Rows 17–24: Ch 2, *sk next sc, sc in next ch-1 sp, ch 1, rep from * across to beg ch-2 sp, sc in beg ch-2 sp, turn.

COLLAR
Row 25: Ch 10 *(for collar)*, sc in 4th ch from hook, ch 1, [sk next ch, sc in next ch, ch 1] 3 times, *sk next sc, sc in next ch-1 sp, ch 1, rep from * across to beg ch-2 sp, sc in beg ch-2 sp, turn.

Row 26: Ch 2, *sk next sc, sc in next ch-1 sp, ch 1, rep from * across to sp formed by beg 3 sk chs, sc in sp, turn.

Rows 27–36: Ch 2, *sk next sc, sc in next ch-1 sp, ch 1, rep from * across to beg ch-2 sp, sc in beg ch-2 sp, turn. Fasten off at end of last row.

2ND SIDE

Rows 1–33: Rep rows 1–33 of First Side.

Row 34: Ch 2, sk next sc, [sc in next ch-1 sp, ch 1, sk next sc, sc in next ch-1 sp, ch 3, sk next 3 sts] 3 times, sc in next ch-1 sp, ch 1, *sk next sc, sc in next ch-1 sp, ch 1, rep from * across to beg ch-2 sp, sc in beg ch-2 sp, turn.

Row 35: Ch 2, *sk next sc, sc in next ch-1 sp, ch 1, rep from * across to next ch-3 sp, [(sc, ch 1, sc) in ch-3 sp, ch 1, sk next sc, sc in next ch-1 sp, ch 1, sk next sc, sc in next ch-1 sp, ch 1] twice, (sc, ch 1, sc) in next ch-3 sp, ch 1, sk next sc, sc in next ch-1 sp, ch 1, sc in beg ch-2 sp, turn.

Row 36: Ch 2, *sk next sc, sc in next ch-1 sp, ch 1, rep from * across to beg ch-2 sp, sc in beg ch-2 sp, turn. Fasten off.

Sew back, shoulder and Collar seams.

SLEEVES

Rnd 1: With size J hook, **join** *(see Pattern Notes)* yarn in any ch-1 sp of 1 armhole, ch 2, *sk next sc, sc in next ch-1 sp, ch 1, rep from * around, join in beg ch-2 sp, turn.

Rnds 2–8: Ch 2, *sc in next ch-1 sp, ch 1, sk next sc, rep from * around to beg ch-2 sp, join in beg ch-2 sp, turn.

Rnds 9–11: With size 7 hook, ch 2, *sc in next ch-1 sp, ch 1, sk next sc, rep from * around to beg ch-2 sp, join in beg ch-2 sp, turn. Fasten off at end of last rnd.

Rep for 2nd Sleeve.

LEGGINGS
Make 2.

Row 1: With size J hook, ch 20, sc in 4th ch from hook, ch 1, *sk next ch, sc in next ch, ch 1, rep from * across to last ch, sc in last ch, turn. *(9 sc)*

Row 2: **Ch 2** *(see Pattern Notes)*, *sk next sc, sc in next ch-1 sp, ch 1, rep from * across to sp formed by beg 3 sk chs, sc in sp, turn.

Rows 3–17: Ch 2, *sc in next ch-1 sp, ch 1, sk next sc, rep from * across to beg ch-2 sp, **join** *(see Pattern Notes)* in beg ch-2 sp, turn.

Fasten off at end of last row.

HAT

Rnd 1: With size J hook, ch 32, **join** *(see Pattern Notes)* in first ch to form ring, ch 2, *sk next ch, sc in next ch, ch 1, rep from * around, join in first ch-2 sp, turn.

Rnds 2–12: **Ch 2** *(see Pattern Notes)*, *sc in next sc, ch 1, sk next sc, rep from * around to beg ch-2 sp, join in beg ch-2 sp, turn. Fasten off at end of last rnd.

TIE
Ch 60. Fasten off.

FINISHING
With yarn, sew buttons opposite buttonholes on Jacket. Sew seam at back of each Legging. Thread Tie through ch-1 sps on rnd 1 of Hat, gather slightly and tie bow. ∎

Fiesta Time

SKILL LEVEL

INTERMEDIATE

FINISHED MEASUREMENT

10 inches long

MATERIALS

- Omega Trigo light (light worsted) weight cotton yarn (3½ oz/295 yds/ 100g per ball):
  1 ball each #273 turquoise, #235 Mexican pink, #283 olive and #267 blue jean
- Size D/3/3.25mm crochet hook or size needed to obtain gauge
- Tapestry needle
- ½-inch buttons: 2

GAUGE

19 sc = 4 inches; 8 rows = 4 inches

PATTERN NOTES

Weave in ends as work progresses.

Join with slip stitch as indicated unless otherwise stated.

Chain-3 at beginning of row counts as first double crochet unless otherwise stated.

Chain-4 at beginning of row counts as first double crochet and chain-1 unless otherwise stated.

SPECIAL STITCH

Shell: (3 dc, ch 1, 3 dc) as indicated in instructions.

DRESS

Row 1: With turquoise, ch 42, 3 dc in 6th ch from hook (5 sk chs counts as first dc and ch-1), ch 1, [sk next 2 chs, 3 dc in next ch, ch 1] 11 times, sk next 2 chs, dc in last ch, do not turn. Fasten off. *(38 dc, 13 ch-1 sps)*

Row 2: Join *(see Pattern Notes)* pink in first ch-1 sp, **ch 3** *(see Pattern Notes)*, 2 dc in same sp, ch 1, 3 dc in next ch-1 sp, ch 1, **shell** *(see Special Stitch)* in next ch-1 sp, [ch 1, 3 dc in next ch-1 sp] twice, ch 1, shell in next ch-1 sp, ch 1, 3 dc in next ch-1 sp, ch 1, shell in next ch-1 sp, [ch 1, 3 dc in next ch-1 sp] twice, ch 1, shell in next ch-1 sp, [ch 1, 3 dc in next ch-1 sp] twice. Fasten off. *(27 dc, 12 ch-1 sps and 4 shells)*

Row 3: Join olive in first st, **ch 4** *(see Pattern Notes)*, [3 dc in next ch-1 sp, ch 1] 16 times, dc in last st. Fasten off olive. *(50 dc, 17 ch-1 sps)*

Row 4: Join blue in first ch-1 sp, ch 3, 2 dc in same sp, ch 1, [3 dc in next ch-1 sp, ch 1] 15 times, 3 dc in last ch-1 sp, turn. *(51 dc, 16 ch-1 sps)*

ARMHOLE SHAPING

Row 5: Ch 4, [3 dc in next ch-1 sp, ch 1] twice, shell in next ch-1 sp, ch 6 *(armhole made)*, sk next 3 3-dc groups, shell in next ch-1 sp, ch 1, [3 dc in next ch-1 sp, ch 1] 4 times, shell in next ch-1 sp, ch 6 *(armhole made)*, sk next 3 3-dc groups, shell in next ch-1 sp, ch 1, [3 dc in next ch-1 sp, ch 1] twice, sk next 2 dc, dc in last dc, turn. *(26 dc, 4 shells, 11 ch-1 sps, 2 ch-6 sps)*

Row 6: Ch 3, *dc in each ch-1 sp and dc across to next ch-6 sp, 6 dc in next ch-6 sp, rep from * once, dc in each dc and ch-1 sp across. *(76 dc)*

Rows 7–16: Ch 3, working in **front lps** *(see Stitch Guide)*, dc in each dc across. Fasten off at end of row 16.

BOTTOM TRIM

Getting Started: Sew back seam from row 8 to row 16, leaving rem rows open for back neck.

Rnd 1: Now working in rnds, join turquoise in first st, ch 3, 2 dc in same st, [ch 1, sk next st, 3 dc in next st] 38 times, ch 1, join in first st. Fasten off. *(117 dc, 39 ch-1 sps)*

Rnd 2: Join pink in first ch-1 sp, ch 3, 2 dc in same sp, shell in each rem ch-1 sp around, join in first st. Fasten off.

Rnd 3: With olive, rep rnd 2. Fasten off.

Rnd 4: With blue, rep rnd 2. Fasten off.

NECK TRIM

Join blue in side of first st of row 7 at back opening, sc evenly sp along row ends of back opening, across opposite side of foundation ch and along row ends of opposite side of back opening.

FINISHING

Sew buttons at top of neck opening. ∎

Hip Hat & Cowl

HOT PINK HAT

SKILL LEVEL

INTERMEDIATE

FINISHED MEASUREMENT
5½ inches in diameter

MATERIALS
- Omega Trigo light (light worsted) weight cotton yarn (3½ oz/295 yds/ 100g per ball):
  1 ball #235 Mexican pink
- Sizes D/3/3.25mm and G/6/4mm crochet hooks or size needed to obtain gauge
- Tapestry needle

GAUGE
With size G hook: Rnds 1–3 = 3½ inches

PATTERN NOTES
Weave in ends as work progresses.

Chain-3 at beginning of round counts as first double crochet unless otherwise stated.

Join with slip stitch as indicated unless otherwise stated.

Chain-2 at beginning of round counts as first single crochet and chain-1 unless otherwise stated.

SPECIAL STITCHES
Beginning shell (beg shell): (2 dc, ch 2, dc) as indicated in instructions.

Shell: (3 dc, ch 2, dc) as indicated in instructions.

HAT

Rnd 1: With size G hook, ch 5, sl st in first ch to form ring, **ch 3** *(see Pattern Notes)*, 9 dc in ring, **join** *(see Pattern Notes)* in 3rd ch of beg ch-3. *(10 dc)*

Rnd 2: Ch 3, **beg shell** *(see Special Stitches)* in first st, **shell** *(see Special Stitches)* in each rem st around, join in 3rd ch of beg ch-3. *(10 shells)*

Rnds 3–10: Sl st in each st to next ch-2 sp, (sl st, beg shell) in same ch-2 sp, shell in each rem ch-2 sp around, join in 3rd ch of beg ch-3, turn.

Rnd 11: Sl st in each st to next ch-2 sp, (sl st, beg shell) in same ch-2 sp, shell in each rem ch-2 sp around, join in 3rd ch of beg ch-3, do not turn.

Rnd 12: Ch 2 *(see Pattern Notes)*, [sc in next dc, ch 1, sk next dc, sc in next ch-2 sp, ch 1, sc in next dc, ch 1, sk next dc] 9 times, sc in next dc, ch 1, sk next dc, sc in next ch-2 sp, ch 1, join in first ch of beg ch-2, turn.

EDGING

Rnds 13–16: With size D hook, ch 2, sc in first ch-2 sp, ch 1, sk next sc, *sc in next ch-2 sp, ch 1, sk next sc, rep from * around, join in beg ch-2 sp, turn. At end of last rnd, fasten off.

TIE

Ch 100. Fasten off.

Fold chain in half, weave through rnds 5–11, pull to gather and tie in bow.

STRIPED COWL

SKILL LEVEL

EASY

FINISHED MEASUREMENT
6 inches in diameter

MATERIALS
- Omega Trigo light (light worsted) weight cotton yarn (3½ oz/295 yds/ 100g per ball):
  1 ball each #273 turquoise, #235 Mexican pink and #224 taupe
- Omega Mimosa fine (sport) weight cotton/rayon yarn (3½ oz/240 yds/ 100g per skein):
  1 skein #83 lime
- Size D/3/3.25mm crochet hook
- Tapestry needle

GAUGE
Gauge is not important for this project.

PATTERN NOTES
Weave in ends as work progresses.

Join with slip stitch as indicated unless otherwise stated.

COWL

Row 1: With turquoise, ch 10, sc in 2nd ch from hook, sc in each rem ch across, turn. *(9 sc)*

Rows 2–5: Ch 1, sc in each st across. At end of last row, fasten off.

Row 6: **Join** *(see Pattern Notes)* lime in first st, ch 1, sc in each st across, turn.

Rows 7–10: Rep rows 2–5. At end of last row, fasten off.

Rows 11–15: Join pink in first st, ch 1, rep rows 6–10. At end of last row, fasten off.

Rows 16–20: Join taupe in first st, ch 1, rep rows 6–10. At end of last row, fasten off.

Rows 21–40: Rep rows 1–20. At end of last row, fasten off.

FINISHING
Twist piece to align last st of row 1 with first st of row 40. Sew ends tog. ∎

Glitter Princess

SKILL LEVEL

INTERMEDIATE

FINISHED MEASUREMENTS

Dress: 9½ inches long

Overskirt/Cape: 11 inches at waist, without ties

Headband: 3 inches wide

MATERIALS

- Omega Trigo light (light worsted) weight cotton yarn (3½ oz/295 yds/ 100g per ball):
    - 2 balls #273 turquoise
- S. Charles Collezione Celine super fine (fingering) weight viscose/ Sinflex® polyester metallic yarn (163 yds/20g per ball):
    - 1 ball #02 titanium
- Sizes E/4/3.5mm, F/5/3.75mm and G/6/4mm crochet hooks or size needed to obtain gauge
- Tapestry needle
- Stitch marker
- ¾-inch buttons: 3
- Hair elastic

GAUGE

With size G hook and 1 strand of turquoise and titanium held tog: 16 dc = 4 inches; 7 rows = 4 inches

PATTERN NOTES

Dress Front is worked in rows then Back is worked on either side of Front.

Weave in ends as work progresses.

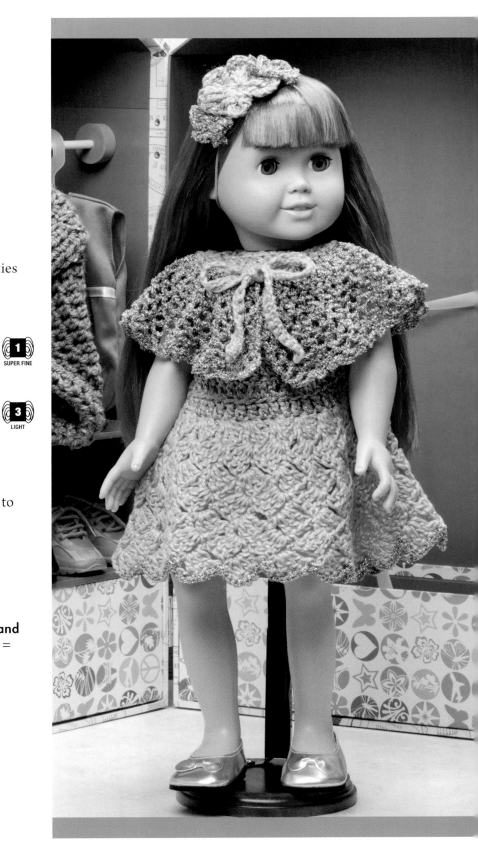

Chain-3 at beginning of row counts as first double crochet unless otherwise stated.

Join with slip stitch as indicated unless otherwise stated.

Chain-2 at beginning of row counts as first single crochet and chain-1 space unless otherwise stated.

Chain-5 at beginning of row counts as first double crochet and chain-2 space unless otherwise stated.

SPECIAL STITCH
Shell: (Sc, ch 3, 3 dc) as indicated in instructions.

DRESS
FRONT
Row 1: With size G hook and with 1 strand turquoise and 1 strand titanium held tog, ch 22, dc in 4th ch from hook (*sk 3 chs count as first dc*), dc in each rem ch across, turn. *(20 dc)*

Rows 2–8: **Ch 3** (*see Pattern Notes*), working in **front lps** (*see Stitch Guide*), dc in each st across, turn.

SHOULDER SHAPING
Row 9: Ch 3, dc in each of next 3 sts, sl st in each of next 12 sts, dc in each of last 4 sts. Fasten off titanium only.

BACK
FIRST SIDE
Note: Turn the work clockwise 90 degrees and work down the side of the front.

Row 1: With size E hook and 1 strand turquoise, sc in top of last st worked in row 9, ch 10, sk next 4 rows (*armhole made*), [sc, ch 1] 6 times evenly sp along rem 5 rows, sc in last row, turn. *(8 sc, 1 ch-10 sp, 6 ch-1 sps)*

Row 2: **Ch 2** (*see Pattern Notes*), *sk next sc, sc in next ch-1 sp, ch 1, rep from * across to ch-10 sp, [sc, ch 1] 5 times in ch-10 sp, sc in last sc, turn.

Row 3–15: Ch 2, *sk next sc, sc in next ch-1 sp, ch 1, rep from * across to beg ch-2 sp, sc in ch-2 sp, turn. Fasten off at end of last row.

2ND SIDE
Rows 1–11: With size G hook and 1 strand turquoise, join in first st of row 9, rep rows 1–11 as for First Side.

Row 12: Ch 2, sk next sc, *sc in next ch-1 sp, ch 3, sk next 3 sts *(buttonhole made)*, [sc in next ch-1 sp, ch 1, sk next sc] twice, rep from * twice, [sc in next ch-1 sp, ch 1, sk next sc] twice, sc in beg ch-2 sp, turn.

Row 13: Ch 2, sk next sc, *(sc, ch 1, sc) in next ch-3 sp, [ch 1, sk next sc, sc in next ch-1 sp] twice, ch 1, rep from * once, (sc, ch 1, sc) in next ch-3 sp, ch 1, sk next sc, sc in next sc, ch 1, sc in beg ch-2 sp. Fasten off.

Sew shoulder seams. Sew buttons opposite buttonholes. Sew 3 sts of Backs tog at waist.

OVERSKIRT
Rnd 1: Now working in rnds with size G hook and 1 strand turquoise, join yarn at center back, ch 1, **shell** *(see Special Stitch)* in same st, work 20 shells evenly sp around waist edge, join in first sc, turn. *(21 shells)*

Rnds 2–8: Sl st in each of next 3 dc, sl st in next ch-3 sp, ch 1, shell in same ch-3 sp, shell in each rem ch-3 sp around, join in first sc, turn. Fasten off at end of last rnd.

Rnd 9: With size E hook and 1 strand titanium, join yarn in first sc, ch 1, sc in same st, *sc in each of next 3 chs, 2 sc in each of next 3 dc, sc in next sc, rep from * around, join in first sc. Fasten off.

OVERSKIRT/CAPE
Row 1: With size E hook and 1 strand titanium, ch 81, sc in 2nd ch from hook, ch 5, [sc in next ch, ch 5] across to last ch, sc in last ch, turn. *(81 sc, 80 ch-5 lps)*

Row 2: Ch 5, sc in first ch-5 lp, *ch 5, sc in next ch-5 lp, rep from * across to last ch-5 lp, ch 2, dc in last sc, turn.

Row 3: *Ch 5, sc in next ch-5 lp, rep from * across, turn.

Rows 4–11: [Rep rows 2 and 3 alternately] 4 times. Fasten off.

WAIST
Row 1: With size E hook and 1 strand turquoise, ch 30, working over foundation ch, [**sc dec** *(see Stitch Guide)* in next 2 ch-5 lps on opposite side of row 1] 40 times, ch 31, turn. *(101 sts)*

Row 2: Sc in 2nd ch from hook, sc in each st across. Fasten off. *(100 sc)*

FLOWER
Make 1 with size G hook and holding 1 strand of turquoise & titanium held tog.

Make 2 with size D hook & 1 strand of titanium.

Rnd 1: Ch 5, join in first ch to form ring, ch 1, [(sc, ch 4, 3 tr, ch 4) in ring] 5 times, join in first sc. Fasten off.

FINISHING
Sew Flowers on hair elastic. ∎

Runway Fashion Dress
Continued from page 2

Rnd 15: **Ch 2** *(see Pattern Notes)*, hdc in each of next 6 sts, 2 hdc in next st, [hdc in each of next 7 sts, 2 hdc in next st] 5 times, join in 2nd ch of beg ch-2. *(54 sts)*

Rnd 16: Ch 2, hdc in each of next 7 sts, 2 hdc in next st, [hdc in each of next 8 sts, 2 hdc in next st] 5 times, join in 2nd ch of beg ch-2. *(60 sts)*

Rnd 17: Ch 2, hdc in each of next 8 sts, 2 hdc in next st, [hdc in each of next 9 sts, 2 hdc in next st] 5 times, join in 2nd ch of beg ch-2. *(66 sts)*

Rnd 18: Ch 2, hdc in each of next 9 sts, 2 hdc in next st, [hdc in each of next 10 sts, 2 hdc in next st] 5 times, join in 2nd ch of beg ch-2. *(72 sts)*

Rnd 19: Ch 2, hdc in each of next 10 sts, 2 hdc in next st, [hdc in each of next 11 sts, 2 hdc in next st] 5 times, join in 2nd ch of beg ch-2. *(78 sts)*

Rnd 20: Ch 2, hdc in each of next 11 sts, 2 hdc in next st, [hdc in each of next 12 sts, 2 hdc in next st] 5 times, join in 2nd ch of beg ch-2. *(84 sts)*

Rnd 21: Ch 2, hdc in same st, hdc in each of next 13 sts, 2 hdc in next st, hdc in each of next 3 sts, ch 20, sl st in 2nd ch from hook, sl st in each rem ch across *(tie made)*, hdc in each of next 10 sts, [2 hdc in next st, hdc in each of next 13 sts] twice, 2 hdc in next st, hdc in each of next 10 sts, ch 20, sl st in 2nd ch from hook, sl st in each rem ch across *(tie made)*, hdc in each of next 3 sts, 2 hdc in next st, hdc in each of next 13 sts, join in 2nd ch of beg ch-2. Fasten off. ■

Today's Cowgirl
Continued from page 7

BAG
Row 1: With size E hook and 1 strand lime, ch 20, sc in 4th ch from hook, ch 1, *sk next ch, sc in next ch, ch 1, rep from * across to last ch, sc in last ch, turn. *(9 sc)*

Row 2: Ch 2 *(see Pattern Notes)*, *sk next sc, sc in next ch-1 sp, ch 1, rep from * across to sp formed by beg 3 sk chs, sc in sp, turn.

Rows 3–24: Ch 2, *sk next sc, sc in next ch-1 sp, ch 1, rep from * across to beg ch-2 sp, sc in beg ch-2 sp, turn.

Row 25: Ch 2, [sk next sc, sc in next ch-1 sp, ch 1] 3 times, sc in next ch-1 sp, (sc, ch 4, **cl**— *see Special Stitches*, ch 10, sl st in each ch across, ch 12, sl st in each ch across, ch 10, sl st in each ch across, ch 4, sc) in next ch-1 sp, [sk next sc, sc in next ch-1 sp, ch 1] 3 times, sc in beg ch-2 sp. Fasten off.

FINISHING
Fold piece in half. With size E hook, join lime at fold, working through both thicknesses, (sc, ch 1) evenly sp across side edge, ch 40 for the strap, (sc, ch 1) evenly sp across opposite side edge to fold. Fasten off. ∎

Snuggly Bear Romper & Hood
Continued from page 9

EDGING
Row 1: With size J hook, **join** *(see Pattern Notes)* yarn in first st of row 23, **ch 2** *(see Pattern Notes)*, [sc, ch 1] 31 times evenly sp along entire edge, ending with sc in last st, turn. *(33 sc, 32 ch-1 sps)*

Row 2: Ch 2, sk first sc, [sc in next ch-1 sp, ch 1, sk next sc] 31 times, sc in last ch-2 sp. Fasten off.

FINISHING
Starting at back of Romper, weave Cord through sc of row 1 of Body. Sew seam at sole of each Foot. Referring to photo for placement, sew one Ear to each side of Hood. Sew button opposite buttonhole on Hood. ∎

STITCH GUIDE

FOR MORE COMPLETE INFORMATION,
VISIT **ANNIESCATALOG.COM/STITCHGUIDE**

STITCH ABBREVIATIONS

beg . . . . begin/begins/beginning
bpdc . . . . back post double crochet
bpsc . . . . .back post single crochet
bptr . . . . .back post treble crochet
CC . . . . contrasting color
ch(s) . . . . .chain(s)
ch- . . . . refers to chain or space
previously made (i.e., ch-1 space)
ch sp(s) . . . . chain space(s)
cl(s) . . . . cluster(s)
cm . . . . centimeter(s)
dc . . . . double crochet (singular/plural)
dc dec . . . . double crochet 2 or more
stitches together, as indicated
dec . . . . decrease/decreases/decreasing
dtr . . . . double treble crochet
ext . . . . .extended
fpdc . . . . front post double crochet
fpsc . . . . front post single crochet
fptr . . . . front post treble crochet
g . . . . .gram(s)
hdc . . . . half double crochet
hdc dec . . . . half double crochet 2 or more
stitches together, as indicated
inc . . . . increase/increases/increasing
lp(s) . . . . .loop(s)
MC . . . . .main color
mm . . . . .millimeter(s)
oz . . . . .ounce(s)
pc . . . . popcorn(s)
rem . . . . .remain/remains/remaining
rep(s) . . . . .repeat(s)
rnd(s) . . . . round(s)
RS . . . . right side
sc . . . . single crochet (singular/plural)
sc dec . . . . .single crochet 2 or more
stitches together, as indicated
sk . . . . .skip/skipped/skipping
sl st(s) . . . . slip stitch(es)
sp(s) . . . . space(s)/spaced
st(s) . . . . stitch(es)
tog . . . . .together
tr . . . . treble crochet
trtr . . . . .triple treble
WS . . . . wrong side
yd(s) . . . . yard(s)
yo . . . . yarn over

YARN CONVERSION

OUNCES TO GRAMS	GRAMS TO OUNCES
1 . . . . 28.4	25 . . . . ⅞
2 . . . . 56.7	40 . . . . 1⅔
3 . . . . 85.0	50 . . . . 1¾
4 . . . . 113.4	100 . . . . 3½

UNITED STATES		UNITED KINGDOM
sl st (slip stitch)	=	sc (single crochet)
sc (single crochet)	=	dc (double crochet)
hdc (half double crochet)	=	htr (half treble crochet)
dc (double crochet)	=	tr (treble crochet)
tr (treble crochet)	=	dtr (double treble crochet)
dtr (double treble crochet)	=	ttr (triple treble crochet)
skip	=	miss

Single crochet decrease (sc dec): (Insert hook, yo, draw lp through) in each of the sts indicated, yo, draw through all lps on hook.

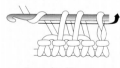

Example of 2-sc dec

Half double crochet decrease (hdc dec): (Yo, insert hook, yo, draw lp through) in each of the sts indicated, yo, draw through all lps on hook.

Example of 2-hdc dec

Reverse single crochet (reverse sc): Ch 1, sk first st, working from left to right, insert hook in next st from front to back, draw up lp on hook, yo and draw through both lps on hook.

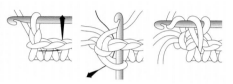

Chain (ch): Yo, pull through lp on hook.

Single crochet (sc): Insert hook in st, yo, pull through st, yo, pull through both lps on hook.

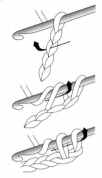

Double crochet (dc): Yo, insert hook in st, yo, pull through st, [yo, pull through 2 lps] twice.

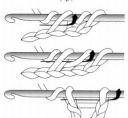

Double crochet decrease (dc dec): (Yo, insert hook, yo, draw lp through, yo, draw through 2 lps on hook) in each of the sts indicated, yo, draw through all lps on hook.

Example of 2-dc dec

Front loop (front lp) Back loop (back lp)

Front Loop   Back Loop

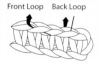

Front post stitch (fp): Back post stitch (bp): When working post st, insert hook from right to left around post of st on previous row.

Back   Front

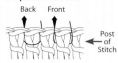

←Post of Stitch

Half double crochet (hdc): Yo, insert hook in st, yo, pull through st, yo, pull through all 3 lps on hook.

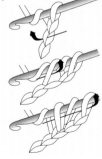

Double treble crochet (dtr): Yo 3 times, insert hook in st, yo, pull through st, [yo, pull through 2 lps] 4 times.

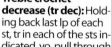

Treble crochet decrease (tr dec): Holding back last lp of each st, tr in each of the sts indicated, yo, pull through all lps on hook.

Example of 2-tr dec

Slip stitch (sl st): Insert hook in st, pull through both lps on hook.

Chain color change (ch color change) Yo with new color, draw through last lp on hook.

Double crochet color change (dc color change) Drop first color, yo with new color, draw through last 2 lps of st.

Treble crochet (tr): Yo twice, insert hook in st, yo, pull through st, [yo, pull through 2 lps] 3 times.

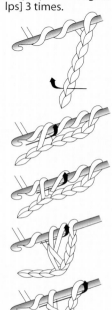

Metric Conversion Charts

METRIC CONVERSIONS

yards	x	.9144	=	metres (m)
yards	x	91.44	=	centimetres (cm)
inches	x	2.54	=	centimetres (cm)
inches	x	25.40	=	millimetres (mm)
inches	x	.0254	=	metres (m)

centimetres	x	.3937	=	inches
metres	x	1.0936	=	yards

INCHES INTO MILLIMETRES & CENTIMETRES (Rounded off slightly)

inches	mm	cm	inches	cm	inches	cm	inches	cm
$1/8$	3	0.3	5	12.5	21	53.5	38	96.5
$1/4$	6	0.6	$5 1/2$	14	22	56	39	99
$3/8$	10	1	6	15	23	58.5	40	101.5
$1/2$	13	1.3	7	18	24	61	41	104
$5/8$	15	1.5	8	20.5	25	63.5	42	106.5
$3/4$	20	2	9	23	26	66	43	109
$7/8$	22	2.2	10	25.5	27	68.5	44	112
1	25	2.5	11	28	28	71	45	114.5
$1 1/4$	32	3.2	12	30.5	29	73.5	46	117
$1 1/2$	38	3.8	13	33	30	76	47	119.5
$1 3/4$	45	4.5	14	35.5	31	79	48	122
2	50	5	15	38	32	81.5	49	124.5
$2 1/2$	65	6.5	16	40.5	33	84	50	127
3	75	7.5	17	43	34	86.5		
$3 1/2$	90	9	18	46	35	89		
4	100	10	19	48.5	36	91.5		
$4 1/2$	115	11.5	20	51	37	94		

KNITTING NEEDLES CONVERSION CHART

Canada/U.S.	0	1	2	3	4	5	6	7	8	9	10	10½	11	13	15
Metric (mm)	2	2¼	2¾	3¼	3½	3¾	4	4½	5	5½	6	6½	8	9	10

CROCHET HOOKS CONVERSION CHART

Canada/U.S.	1/B	2/C	3/D	4/E	5/F	6/G	8/H	9/I	10/J	10½/K	N
Metric (mm)	2.25	2.75	3.25	3.5	3.75	4.25	5	5.5	6	6.5	9.0